Learn-a-Stitch
CROCHET
SCARVES™

Table of Contents

Carnelian Stripe Scarf,
page 4

Marvel
Mosaic
Scarf,
page 12

Snowbird Scarf, *page 8*

Crazy for Cables Scarf

Design by Amy D. Brewer

Skill Level

Finished Measurements

7 inches wide x 64 inches long

Materials

- Scheepjes Stone Washed XL medium (Aran) weight cotton/acrylic yarn (1¾ oz/82 yds/50g per ball):
    6 balls #848 corundum ruby
- Size J/10/6mm crochet hook or size needed to obtain gauge
- Tapestry needle

Gauge

First 8 rows of pattern = 4 inches

Scarf

Row 1 (WS): Ch 25, hdc in 2nd ch from hook and in each ch across, turn. *(24 hdc)*

Row 2 (RS): Ch 1, hdc in each of first 2 sts, **fpdc** *(see Stitch Guide)* around each of next 2 sts, hdc in each of next 2 sts, sk next 2 sts, **fptr** *(see Stitch Guide)* around each of next 2 sts, working in front of last 2 fptr sts, fptr around each of 2 sts just sk, hdc in each of next 4 sts, sk next 2 sts, fptr around each of next 2 sts, working in front of last 2 fptr sts, fptr around each of 2 sts just sk, hdc in each of next 2 sts, fpdc around each of next 2 sts, hdc in each of last 2 sts, turn.

Row 3: Ch 1, hdc in each of first 2 sts, **bpdc** *(see Stitch Guide)* around each of next 2 sts, hdc in each of next 2 sts, bpdc around each of next 2 sts, sk next 2 sts, tr in each of next 2 sts, working behind last 2 tr sts, **bptr** *(see Stitch Guide)* around each of 2 sts just sk, sk next 2 sts, bptr around each of next 2 sts, working in front of last 2 bptr sts, tr in each of 2 sts just sk, [bpdc around each of next 2 sts, hdc in each of next 2 sts] twice, turn.

Row 4: Ch 1, hdc in each of first 2 sts, [fpdc around each of next 2 sts, hdc in each of next 2 sts] twice, sk next 2 sts, fptr around each of next 2 sts, working in front of last 2 fptr sts, fptr around each of 2 sts just sk, [hdc in each of next 2 sts, fpdc around each of next 2 sts] twice, hdc in each of last 2 sts, turn.

Row 5: Ch 1, hdc in each of first 2 sts, [bpdc around each of next 2 sts, hdc in each of next 2 sts] twice, bpdc around each of next 4 sts, [hdc in each of next 2 sts, bpdc around each of next 2 sts] twice, hdc in each of last 2 sts, turn.

Row 6: Rep row 4.

Row 7: Ch 1, hdc in each of first 2 sts, bpdc around each of next 2 sts, hdc in each of next 2 sts, bpdc around each of next 2 sts, sk next 2 sts, bptr around each of next 2 sts, working in front of last 2 bptr sts, tr in each of 2 sts just sk, sk next 2 sts, tr in next 2 sts, working behind last 2 tr sts, bptr around each of 2 sts just sk, [bpdc around each of next 2 sts, hdc in each of next 2 sts] twice, turn.

Row 8: Rep row 2.

Row 9: Ch 1, hdc in each of first 2 sts, bpdc around each of next 2 sts, hdc in each of next 2 sts, bpdc around each of next 4 sts, hdc in each of next 4 sts, bpdc around each of next 4 sts, hdc in each of next 2 sts, bpdc around each of next 2 sts, hdc in each of last 2 sts, turn.

Rows 10–121: [Rep rows 2–9] 14 times.

Rows 122–128: Rep rows 2–8.

Row 129: Sl st in each st across. Fasten off. ●

Carnelian Stripe Scarf

Design by Lena Skvagerson for Annie's Signature Designs

Skill Level

 EASY

Finished Measurements

8 inches x 74 inches

Materials

- Scheepjes Stone Washed XL medium (Aran) weight cotton/acrylic yarn (1¾ oz/82 yds/50g per ball):
    2 balls each #844 boulder opal (brown), #863 carnelian (red), #856 coral (orange), and #852 lemon quartz (yellow)
- Size J/10/6mm crochet hook or size needed to obtain gauge
- Tapestry needle

4 MEDIUM

Gauge

11 3-dc groups = 12 inches

Stripe Pattern

Work 1 row in each color as follows:

*boulder opal, carnelian, coral, lemon quartz, rep colors from *.

Cut and leave 4-inch tail, weave into stripe of same color later.

Scarf

Row 1: With boulder opal, ch 204 loosely, 3 dc in 6th ch from hook *(sk chs count as turning ch sp)*, [sk next 2 chs, 3 dc in next ch] across changing to **next color** *(see Stripe Pattern)* in last dc of last 3-dc group, turn. *(1 turning ch, 67 3-dc groups)*

Row 2: Ch 4 *(counts as turning ch sp)*, 3 dc between first 2 3-dc groups, [3 dc between next 2 3-dc groups] across ending with 3 dc in turning ch sp, changing to next color in last dc of last 3-dc group, turn.

Rows 3–13: [Rep row 2] 11 times.

Picot Edge

Rnd 1: With carnelian, ch 3, dc in 3rd ch from hook, sc between first 2 3-dc groups, [ch 3, dc in 3rd ch from hook, sc between next 2 3-dc groups] across ending with sc in turning ch sp, ch 3, dc in 3rd ch from hook, sc in same turning ch sp as last sc, working across short end of scarf, [ch 3, dc in 3rd ch from hook, sc in next turning ch sp] 6 times, changing to lemon quartz in last sc, ch 3, dc in 3rd ch from hook, sc in same turning ch sp as last sc, working across long side of scarf, [ch 3, dc in 3rd ch from hook, sc in next ch sp] across ending with sc in turning ch sp, ch 3, dc in 3rd ch from hook, sc in same turning ch sp as last sc, working across short end of scarf, [ch 3, dc in 3rd ch from hook, sc in next turning ch sp] 5 times, ch 3, dc in 3rd ch from hook, join in same st as beg ch-3. Fasten off. ●

Smokey
Moon
Scarf

Design by Lena Skvagerson
for Annie's Signature Designs

Skill Level

 EASY

Finished Measurements

7½ inches x 60 inches

Materials

- Scheepjes Stone Washed XL medium (Aran) weight cotton/acrylic yarn (1¾ oz/82 yds/50g per ball):
  - 3 balls #842 smokey quartz (A)
  - 2 balls each #841 moon stone (B) and #850 garnet (C)
- Size J/10/6mm crochet hook or size needed to obtain gauge
- Tapestry needle

Gauge

16 sts = 5 inches/10 cm

Pattern Notes

When working into a stitch 2 rows below, work over the chain-2 space on row below.

Carry alternating colors along the edge.

Scarf

Row 1: With A, ch 25, hdc in 3rd ch from hook *(sk chs count as 1 hdc)*, hdc in next ch, [ch 2, sk next 2 chs, hdc in each of next 2 chs] 5 times, hdc in last ch, turn. *(14 hdc, 5 ch-2 sps)*

Row 2: Ch 1, sc in first hdc, ch 2, sk next 2 hdc, [hdc in each of next 2 chs **2 rows below** *(see Pattern Notes)*, ch 2, sk next 2 hdc] 5 times, sc in last st, turn. *(2 sc, 10 hdc, 6 ch-2 sps)*

Row 3: Ch 1, sc in first sc, [hdc in each of next 2 hdc 2 rows below, ch 2, sk next 2 hdc] 5 times, hdc in each of next 2 hdc 2 rows below, sk last sc, sc in turning ch-1, turn. *(2 sc, 12 hdc, 5 ch-2 sps)*

Row 4: Ch 1, sc in first sc, ch 2, sk next 2 hdc, [hdc in each of next 2 hdc 2 rows below, ch 2, sk next 2 hdc] 5 times, sk last sc, sc in turning ch-1, turn. *(2 sc, 10 hdc, 6 ch-2 sps)*

Rows 5–20: [Rep rows 3 and 4] 8 times *(piece should be 6 inches long)*.

Continue rep rows 3 and 4 alternating colors on every row in the following order B, C, A, until piece measures 54 inches from beg ending with a row in A. Fasten off B and C.

Continue rep rows 3 and 4 with A until piece measures 59½ inches, ending with row 3.

Last row: Ch 1, sc in first sc, sc in each of next 2 hdc, [hdc in each of next 2 hdc 2 rows below, sc in each of next 2 hdc] 5 times, sk last sc, sc in turning ch-1. Fasten off. *(14 sc, 10 hdc)*

Tassels

Make 4.

With A, cut fifteen 9-inch strands.

Tie a strand in A tight around center of strands and leave tails long.

Fold strands double and wrap a strand of Color B tight around strands approximately ¾ inch from fold, and tie a tight knot.

Then wrap a strand of C tight around strands right below the wrap with B, and tie a tight knot.

Trim ends even.

Attach 1 tassel in each corner of the scarf. ●

Snowbird Scarf

Design by Lena Skvagerson
for Annie's Signature Designs

Skill Level

 EASY

Finished Measurements

8 inches x 66 inches

Materials

- Scheepjes Stone Washed XL medium (Aran) weight cotton/acrylic yarn (1¾ oz/82 yds/50g per ball):
    5 balls #845 blue apatite
- Size J/10/6mm crochet hook or size needed to obtain gauge
- Tapestry needle

Gauge

13 sts in pattern = 4 inches

Pattern Notes

Weave in loose ends as work progresses.

Chain-2 at beginning of rounds counts as first half double crochet unless otherwise stated.

Chain-3 at beginning of rounds counts as first double crochet unless otherwise stated.

Special Stitch

Bobble: [Yo, insert hook in indicated st, yo, draw through, yo, draw through 2 lps on hook] 5 times, yo, draw through all 6 lps on hook.

Scarf

Row 1 (RS): Ch 27, dc in 4th ch from hook and in each ch across, turn. *(25 dc)*

Row 2: Ch 2 *(see Pattern Notes)*, **bpdc** *(see Stitch Guide)* around post of next st, [**fpdc** *(see Stitch Guide)* around post of next st, bpdc around post of next st] 11 times, hdc in last st, turn. *(22 post sts, 2 hdc)*

Row 3: Ch 2, fpdc around post of next st, [bpdc around post of next st, fpdc around post of next st] 11 times, hdc in last st, turn.

Row 4: Ch 3 *(counts as first hdc and ch-1 sp)*, sk next st, hdc in next st, [ch 1, sk next st, hdc in next st] across, turn. *(13 hdc, 12 ch-1 sps)*

Row 5: Ch 2, hdc in first ch-1 sp, 2 hdc in each ch-1 sp across to last sp, 2 hdc in last sp, hdc in 2nd ch of turning ch-3, turn. *(25 hdc)*

Row 6: Ch 3 *(see Pattern Notes)*, dc in 3rd lp (in the front) of each hdc across to turning ch, dc in top of turning ch, turn. *(25 dc)*

Rows 7 & 8: Rep Rows 4 and 5.

Row 9: Ch 3, working in back lp of each hdc across, dc in each of next 2 sts, **bobble** *(see Special Stitch)* in next st, [dc in each of next 5 sts, bobble in next st] 3 times, dc in each of next 2 sts, dc in top of turning ch, turn. *(4 bobbles, 21 dc)*

Rows 10–14: Rep rows 4–8.

Row 15: Ch 3, working in back lp of each hdc across, [dc in each of next 5 sts, bobble in next st] 3 times, dc in each of next 5 sts, dc in top of turning ch, turn. *(3 bobbles, 22 dc)*

Rows 16–111: [Rep rows 4–15] 8 times.

Rows 112–115: [Rep rows 4–7]

Row 116: Ch 3, dc in first ch-1 sp, 2 dc in each ch-1 sp across to last sp, 2 dc in last sp, dc in 2nd ch of turning ch-3, turn. *(25 dc)*

Row 117: Ch 2, fpdc around post of next st, [bpdc around post of next st, fpdc around post of next st] 11 times, hdc in last st, turn.

Row 118: Ch 2, bpdc around post of next st, [fpdc around post of next st, bpdc around post of next st] 11 times, hdc in last st. Fasten off. *(22 post sts, 2 hdc)* ●

November Lights Scarf

Design by Kenneth Cormier

Skill Level

 EASY

Finished Measurements

7½ inches x 66 inches

Materials

- Scheepjes Stone Washed XL medium (Aran) weight cotton/acrylic yarn (1¾ oz/82 yds/50g per ball):
    4 balls #854 crystal quartz
- Size J/10/6mm crochet hook or size needed to obtain gauge
- Tapestry needle

Gauge

First 7 rows = 4 inches

Pattern Notes

Weave in loose ends as work progresses.

Chain-6 at beginning of row counts as first treble crochet and chain-2 unless otherwise stated.

Chain-3 at beginning of row counts as first double crochet unless otherwise stated.

Scarf

Row 1 (RS): Ch 26, sc in 2nd ch from hook and in next ch, [ch 5, sk next 5 chs, sc in each of next 3 chs] twice, ch 5, sk next 5 chs, sc in each of last 2 chs, turn. *(10 sc, 3 ch-5 sps)*

Row 2: Ch 1, sc in first sc, *ch 3, sk next sc, 3 dc in next ch-5 sp, ch 3, sk next sc, sc in next sc, rep from * across, turn. *(9 dc, 4 sc, 6 ch-3 sps)*

Row 3: Ch 6 *(see Pattern Notes)*, sk first ch-3 sp, sc in each of first 3 dc, [ch 5, sk each of next ch-3 sp, next sc, and next ch-3 sp, sc in each of next 3 dc] twice, ch 2, sk last ch-3 sp, tr in last sc, turn. *(2 tr, 9 sc, 2 ch-5 sps, 2 ch-2 sps)*

Row 4: Ch 3 *(see Pattern Notes)*, dc in ch-2 sp, *ch 3, sk next sc, sc in next sc, ch 3, sk next sc**, 3 dc in next ch-5 sp, rep from * across, ending last rep at **, working in turning ch-6, sk 2 chs, dc in each of next 2 chs, turn. *(10 dc, 3 sc, 6 ch-3 sps)*

Row 5: Ch 1, sc in each of first 2 dc, *ch 5, sk each of next ch-3 sp, next sc, and next ch-3 sp**, sc in each of next 3 dc, rep from * across, ending last rep at **, sc in next dc, sc in top of beg ch-3, turn. *(10 sc, 3 ch-5 sps)*

Rows 6–113: [Rep Rows 2–5 consecutively] 27 times. At end of last row, fasten off.

Fringe

Cut 60 14-inch strands.

For each Fringe, hold 10 strands tog and fold length in half.

Insert hook from WS in ch-5 sp at end of Scarf, pull folded end through, pull ends through fold, pull ends to tighten knot. Work Fringe in each ch-5 sp across each short end. Trim ends even to desired length. ●

Marvel Mosaic Scarf

Design by Lena Skvagerson
for Annie's Signature Designs

Skill Level

 INTERMEDIATE

Finished Measurements

9 inches x 65 inches

Materials
- Scheepjes Stone Washed XL medium (Aran) weight cotton/acrylic yarn (1¾ oz/82 yds/50g per ball):
    4 balls each #849 yellow jasper (A) and #841 moon stone (B)
- Size J/10/6mm crochet hook or size needed to obtain gauge
- Tapestry needle

Gauge

10 sts = 4 inches, 14 rows = 4 inches

Pattern Notes

Weave in ends as work progresses.

Each color is used for 2 rows; the color on your hook when you turn at the end of a row is the color you will use for the next row.

Carry yarn up the sides when not in use.

Special Stitch

Double crochet in next skipped stitch (dc in next sk st): Working in front of ch-2 sp, dc in next skipped st 3 rows below.

Scarf

Row 1 (RS): With A ch 24, sc in 2nd ch from hook and in each ch across, turn. *(23 sc)*

Row 2 (WS): Ch 1, sc in each sc across, **changing to B** *(see illustration)* in last sc, turn.

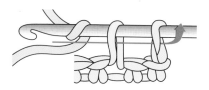

Single Crochet Color Change

Row 3: Ch 1, sc in first sc, [sc in each of next 2 sc, ch 2, sk next sc, sc in each of next 5 sc, ch 2, sk next sc, sc in next sc] twice, sc in each of last 2 sc, turn.

Row 4: Ch 1, sc in each of first 2 sc, [sc in next sc, ch 2, sk next sp, sc in each of next 5 sc, ch 2, sk next sp, sc in each of next 2 sc] across, changing to color A sc in last sc, turn.

Row 5: Ch 1, sc in first sc, [sc in next sc, ch 2, sk next sc, **dc in next sk st** *(see Special Stitch)*, sc in each of next 2 sc, ch 2, sk next sc, sc in each of next 2 sc, dc in next sk st, ch 2, sk next st] across, sc in each of last 2 sc, turn.

Row 6: Ch 1, sc in each of first 2 sc, [(ch 2, sk next sp, sc in each of next 3 sts) twice, ch 2, sk next sp, sc in next sc] across, changing to color B sc in last sc, turn.

Row 7: Ch 1, sc in first sc, [ch 2, sk next sc, dc in next sk st, sc in each of next 2 sc, ch 2, sk next sc, dc in next sk st, ch 2, sk next st, sc in each of next 2 sc, dc in next sk st] across, ch 2, sk next st, sc in last sc, turn.

Row 8: Ch 1, sc in first sc, ch 2, sk next sp, [sc in each of next 3 sts, ch 2, sk next sp, sc in next st, ch 2, sk next sp, sc in each of next 3 sts, ch 2, sk next sp] across, changing to color A sc in last sc, turn.

Row 9: Ch 1, sc in first sc, [dc in next sk st, sc in each of next 2 sc, ch 2, sk next sc, dc in next sk st, sc in next sc, dc in next sk st, ch 2, sk next st, sc in each of next 2 sc] across, dc in next sk st, sc in last sc, turn.

Row 10: Ch 1, sc in each of first 2 sts, [sc in each of next 2 sc, ch 2, sk next sp, sc in each of next 3 sts, ch 2, sk next sp, sc in each of next 3 sts] across, changing to color B sc in last sc, turn.

Row 11: Ch 1, sc in first sc, [sc in each of next 2 sc, ch 2, sk next sc, dc in next sk st, sc in each of next 3 sc, dc in next sk st, ch 2, sk next sc, sc in next sc] twice, sc in each of last 2 sc, turn.

Rows 12–211: [Rep rows 4–11] 25 times.

Row 212–216: Rep rows 4–8.

Row 217: Ch 1, sc in first sc, [dc in next sk st, sc in each of next 3 sc, dc in next sk st, sc in next sc, dc in next sk st, sc in each of next 3 sc] across, dc in next sk st, sc in last sc, turn.

Row 218: Ch 1, sc in each st across, turn.

Row 219: Sl st in each st across. Fasten off. ●

Holiday Sparkle Scarf

Design by
Joyce Geisler

Skill Level

 EASY

Finished Measurements

Without fringe: 6½ inches x 67 inches

With fringe: 6½ inches x 87 inches

Materials

- Scheepjes Stone Washed XL medium (Aran) weight cotton/acrylic yarn (1¾ oz/82 yds/50g per ball):
    5 balls #871 axinite
- Size J/10/6mm crochet hook or size needed to obtain gauge
- Tapestry needle

4 MEDIUM

Gauge

6 rows = 7½ inches

Pattern Notes

All X-stitches are worked in 2 chains or 2 chain-1 spaces. Instructions in rows 1 and 3 indicate the first chain or space in which to begin the stitch. Next X-stitch begins in same chain or chain space as last X-stitch made.

Weave in loose ends as work progresses.

Chain-5 counts as first double treble crochet unless otherwise stated.

Special Stitches

Foundation X-stitch (foundation X-st): Yo twice, insert hook in indicated ch, yo, draw through, yo, draw through 2 lps on hook *(first leg made)*, yo, sk next 2 chs, insert hook in next ch, yo, draw through, [yo, draw through 2 lps on hook] 4 times *(2nd leg made)*, ch 2, dc around post of first leg.

X-stitch (X-st): Yo twice, insert hook in indicated ch-1 sp, yo, draw through, yo, draw through 2 lps on hook *(first leg made)*, yo, insert hook in next ch-1 sp, yo, draw through, [yo, draw through 2 lps on hook] 4 times *(2nd leg made)*, ch 2, dc around post of first leg.

Scarf

Row 1: Ch 27 loosely, **foundation X-st** *(see Special Stitches and Pattern Notes)* in 7th ch from hook *(beg sk chs count as first dtr and sk ch)*, [foundation X-st in last ch worked] 5 times, sk next ch, **dtr** *(see Stitch Guide)* in last ch, turn. *(6 foundation X-sts, 2 dtr)*

Row 2: Ch 5 *(see Pattern Notes)*, dtr in dc of first X-st, [ch 1, 2 dtr in ch-2 sp of X-st] 6 times, ch 1, dtr in last leg of last X-st and in top of turning ch, turn. *(16 dtr, 7 ch-1 sps)*

Row 3: Ch 5, **X-st** *(see Special Stitches)* in first ch-1 sp, [X-st in last ch-1 sp worked] 5 times, dtr in top of turning ch, turn. *(6 X-sts, 2 dtr)*

Rows 4–53: [Rep rows 2 and 3] 25 times. Fasten off.

Finishing

Fringe

Cut 6 pieces of yarn 24 inches long. Hold strands tog, fold in half and pull up lp of fringe in corner sp before first X-st, pull ends of yarn through lp and pull tightly.

Rep fringe in sp between each X-st and in corner sp on each short edge.

Block scarf and trim fringe as desired. ●

Annie's® Published by Annie's, 306 East Parr Road, Berne, IN 46711. Printed in USA. Copyright © 2021 Annie's. All rights reserved. This publication may not be reproduced in part or in whole without written permission from the publisher.

RETAIL STORES: If you would like to carry this publication or any other Annie's publication, visit AnniesWSL.com.

Every effort has been made to ensure that the instructions in this publication are complete and accurate. We cannot, however, take responsibility for human error, typographical mistakes or variations in individual work. Please visit AnniesCustomerService.com to check for pattern updates.

ISBN: 978-1-64025-534-0
1 2 3 4 5 6 7 8 9

STITCH GUIDE

STITCH ABBREVIATIONS

beg . . . . begin/begins/beginning
bpdc . . . . back post double crochet
bpsc . . . . .back post single crochet
bptr . . . . .back post treble crochet
CC . . . . contrasting color
ch(s) . . . . .chain(s)
ch- . . . . refers to chain or space
previously made (i.e., ch-1 space)
ch sp(s) . . . . chain space(s)
cl(s) . . . . cluster(s)
cm . . . . centimeter(s)
dc . . . . double crochet (singular/plural)
dc dec . . . . double crochet 2 or more
stitches together, as indicated
dec . . . . decrease/decreases/decreasing
dtr . . . . double treble crochet
ext . . . . .extended
fpdc . . . . front post double crochet
fpsc . . . . front post single crochet
fptr . . . . front post treble crochet
g . . . . .gram(s)
hdc . . . . half double crochet
hdc dec . . . . .half double crochet 2 or more
stitches together, as indicated
inc . . . . increase/increases/increasing
lp(s) . . . . .loop(s)
MC . . . . .main color
mm . . . . millimeter(s)
oz . . . . .ounce(s)
pc . . . . .popcorn(s)
rem . . . . .remain/remains/remaining
rep(s) . . . . .repeat(s)
rnd(s) . . . . round(s)
RS . . . . right side
sc . . . . single crochet (singular/plural)
sc dec . . . . .single crochet 2 or more
stitches together, as indicated
sk . . . . .skip/skipped/skipping
sl st(s) . . . . slip stitch(es)
sp(s) . . . . space(s)/spaced
st(s) . . . . stitch(es)
tog . . . . .together
tr . . . . treble crochet
trtr . . . . .triple treble
WS . . . . wrong side
yd(s) . . . . yard(s)
yo . . . . yarn over

YARN CONVERSION

OUNCES TO GRAMS	GRAMS TO OUNCES
1 . . . . 28.4	25 . . . . ⅞
2 . . . . 56.7	40 . . . . 1⅔
3 . . . . 85.0	50 . . . . 1¾
4 . . . . 113.4	100 . . . . 3½

UNITED STATES		UNITED KINGDOM
sl st (slip stitch)	=	sc (single crochet)
sc (single crochet)	=	dc (double crochet)
hdc (half double crochet)	=	htr (half treble crochet)
dc (double crochet)	=	tr (treble crochet)
tr (treble crochet)	=	dtr (double treble crochet)
dtr (double treble crochet)	=	ttr (triple treble crochet)
skip	=	miss

Single crochet decrease (sc dec): (Insert hook, yo, draw lp through) in each of the sts indicated, yo, draw through all lps on hook.

Example of 2-sc dec

Half double crochet decrease (hdc dec): (Yo, insert hook, yo, draw lp through) in each of the sts indicated, yo, draw through all lps on hook.

Example of 2-hdc dec

Reverse single crochet (reverse sc): Ch 1, sk first st, working from left to right, insert hook in next st from front to back, draw up lp on hook, yo and draw through both lps on hook.

Chain (ch): Yo, pull through lp on hook.

Single crochet (sc): Insert hook in st, yo, pull through st, yo, pull through both lps on hook.

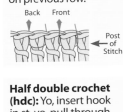

Double crochet (dc): Yo, insert hook in st, yo, pull through st, [yo, pull through 2 lps] twice.

Front loop (front lp) Back loop (back lp)

Front Loop   Back Loop

Front post stitch (fp): Back post stitch (bp): When working post st, insert hook from right to left around post of st on previous row.

Back   Front

Post of Stitch

Half double crochet (hdc): Yo, insert hook in st, yo, pull through st, yo, pull through all 3 lps on hook.

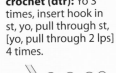

Double treble crochet (dtr): Yo 3 times, insert hook in st, yo, pull through st, [yo, pull through 2 lps] 4 times.

Slip stitch (sl st): Insert hook in st, pull through both lps on hook.

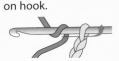

Chain color change (ch color change) Yo with new color, draw through last lp on hook.

Double crochet color change (dc color change) Drop first color, yo with new color, draw through last 2 lps of st.

Treble crochet (tr): Yo twice, insert hook in st, yo, pull through st, [yo, pull through 2 lps] 3 times.

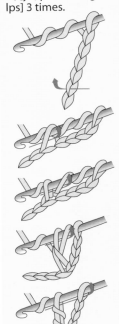

Double crochet decrease (dc dec): (Yo, insert hook, yo, draw lp through, yo, draw through 2 lps on hook) in each of the sts indicated, yo, draw through all lps on hook.

Example of 2-dc dec

Treble crochet decrease (tr dec): Holding back last lp of each st, tr in each of the sts indicated, yo, pull through all lps on hook.

Example of 2-tr dec